# MY BeSt Friend JeSuS!

A SeCret Keeper GiRL Bible Study

# MY BeSt Friend JeSuS!

How to Meditate on God's Truth about Friendship

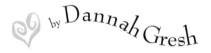 by Dannah Gresh

Moody Publishers
**CHICAGO**

© 2008 by

DANNAH GRESH

The Living Bible was my favorite translation of the Bible when I was about eight. It's easy to understand and fun to read. For language simplicity, I have used the New Living Translation in this Secret Keeper Girl Bible study.

Quotations from the New Living Translation are taken from the *Holy Bible, New Living Translation,* copyright © 1996. Used by permission of Tyndale House Publishers, Inc., Wheaton, Illinois 60189, U.S.A. All rights reserved.

All Web sites and phone numbers listed herein are accurate at the time of writing, but may change in the future or cease to exist. The listing of Web site references and resources does not imply publisher endorsement of the site's entire contents.

ISBN: 978-0-8024-8701-8

Book Cover and Interior Design: www.DesignbyJulia.com
SKG Illustrations, pages 6, 7, 69-72: Andy Mylin
Some images/photographs: © iStock.com and © JupiterImages.com
Cover photograph of jumping girl: © S Tiplyashin / iStock.com
Cover photograph of singing girl: © Steve Tressler, Mountain View Studios

We hope you like this book from Moody Publishers. We want to give you books that help you think and figure out what truth really looks like. If you liked this and want more information, you and/or your mom can go to www.moodypublishers.com or write to . . .

Moody Publishers
820 N. LaSalle Boulevard
Chicago, IL 60610

1 3 5 7 9 10 8 6 4 2

*Printed in the United States of America*

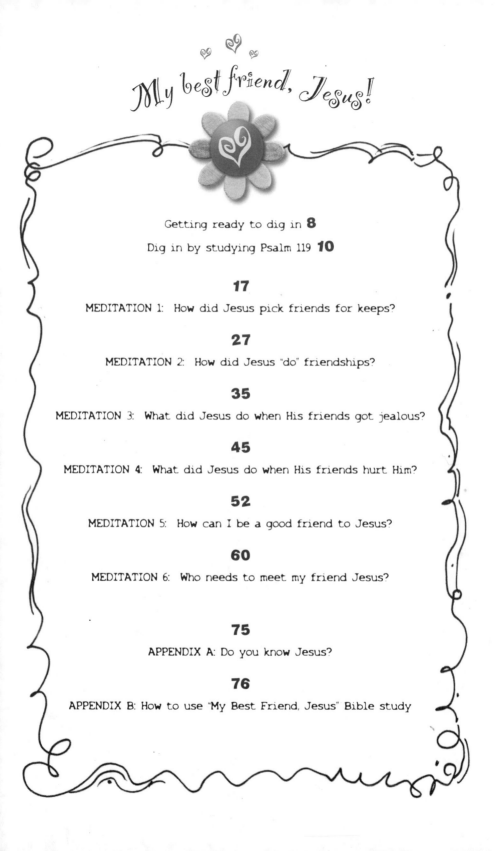

# My best friend, Jesus!

# Hi, Secret Keeper Girl!

When I was eight years old, my mom gave me my first Bible study tool. It was an itty, bitty book that helped me understand one little piece of the Bible each day. I loved it! I don't think I've ever listened more closely to God than during those—my first—years of Bible study.

You're not too young to dig into God's Word!

Secret Keeper Girl stuff may be the most fun you'll ever having digging into God's Word. From our crazy stage events to the fun-filled mother-daughter date kits to this Bible study, I want you to have fun. But I also want all things Secret Keeper Girl to be filled with God's truth from the Bible. This book is your biggest dig yet. It enables you to do your own studying. That means that it *won't* be fun like "I-just-won-the helium-saucers-contest-at-the-SKG-event" kind of fun. You have to put some work in to feel the thrill in your belly for the kind of fun I'm talking about!

It's kind of like being on-site at a great archaeological dig. You dig and dig and dig until your fingers have blisters and your muscles might burst. Then, you see something glimmering in the dust. You clear the remaining pebbles and dirt away and . . . oh my . . . you've just found a golden treasure. You whoop and holler because all the hard work of digging has been forgotten in the thrill of discovery!

That's what studying the Bible can feel like.

I want to help you to love digging into the Bible, so you will do it your whole life long.

Ready for some fun? Roll up your sleeves. Let's start digging.

Dannah

## Getting Ready to Dig In

# *An Introduction to My Best Friend, Jesus!*

Each Secret Keeper Girl Bible study uses the powerful skill of *meditation*. So, before you get into the great subject of friendship and your Best Friend, Jesus, let me take a little time to introduce you to meditation.

### What Is Meditation?

Well, you might think it's some crazy, weird thing you do while sitting cross-legged in a yoga position and humming. That's not true at all. That kind of meditation is just a sad fake for God's original. Let me see if I can help you get an idea of what God thinks meditation should look like.

Some Christians are really rigid about studying, studying, studying the Bible!

**STUDIER**

Some Christians are so consumed with praying all the time, they never study!

**PRAY-ER**

The risk for the **STUDIER** is that her faith gets stuck in her head. She never has the *heart* to follow God because she is always arguing or defending what she *thinks* about God.

The risk for the **PRAY-ER** is that her faith is all about her heart. She makes decisions to follow God based on how she *feels* and forgets to think about what God has already told her in His written Word. (God will never ask you to do something that disagrees with the Bible.)

But then there's a third type of person. A **MEDITATOR** studies the Bible and then asks God to help her understand it while she prays. A wise pastor once told me that meditation is what happens when studying and praying crash into each other!

## MEDITATOR

I want to teach you to meditate. You don't need a yoga mat! But you do need these things:

**1.** Your Bible (You won't actually use it a lot, but that's because I'm keeping this Bible study simple. All the verses you'll need are printed right in this book. But, I want you to get in the habit of having your very own treasured Bible on hand!)

**2.** This copy of *My Best Friend, Jesus!*

**3.** Some colored markers or pencils

These are your meditation tools. Got 'em? OK. Let's just get them warmed up by practicing meditation.

## Dig in by Studying
### Psalm 119

Throughout this book, you'll see this symbol inviting you to "dig in." This means you are about to *study* God's Word, kind of like an archaeologist studies the ground to uncover mysteries, secrets, and stories. So, plop on your hard hat  and get ready to dig. Let's give it a try, OK?

Let's do a little digging to see if God really does want us to practice meditation. After all, you shouldn't take my word for it. Psalm 119 is the loooooongest chapter in the Bible, and it's all *about* the Bible. I wonder if it talks about meditation? Let's find out. Read the Bible verses below with your pink marker in hand. **Circle the word "meditate" in pink every time it shows up.**

### PSALM 119

"Even princes sit and speak against me, but I will

meditate on your principles." (v. 23)

"Help me understand the meaning of your commandments, and I will

meditate on your wonderful miracles." (v. 27)

"I honor and love your commands. I meditate on your principles." (v. 48)

"I will meditate on your age-old laws; O Lord, they comfort me." (v. 52)

"Sustain me, and I will be saved; then I will meditate on

your principles continually." (v. 117)

So, does God want us to meditate? The answer is yes. The longest chapter in the Bible mentions it at least five times. Cool! But, just *what* does He want us to meditate on? **Grab your purple marker. Circle any words in Psalm 119 that answer that question with purple.**

Now, fill in the blanks below by writing what we are supposed to meditate on, based on what you circled in purple.

**1.** . . . . . . . . . . . . . . . . . . . . . . . . . . . . .     **2.** . . . . . . . . . . . . . . . . . . . . . . . . . . . . . .

**3.** . . . . . . . . . . . . . . . . . . . . . . . . . . .     **4.** . . . . . . . . . . . . . . . . . . . . . . . . . . . . . .

We are supposed to meditate on God's principles (or basic rules), commandments, miracles, and age-old laws. Where can you find those things? In the Bible. Meditation always begins with studying the Bible, God's written Word to us.

How does it end? Let's take a peek. This is kind of like turning to the back page of your favorite Secret Keeper Girl fiction book to see how it ends. I don't recommend that if you're reading one of those, but in this case it'll give you determination to put the hard work into this Bible study.

**Read the following verse and use your blue marker to circle the end result of meditation.**

"Study this Book of the Law continually. Meditate on it day

and night so you may be sure to obey all that is written in it.

Only then will you succeed." (Joshua 1:8)

What happens when we meditate on God's Word? We succeed. In fact, God makes a pretty bold promise to us. *Only then* will we succeed. Meditating on God's Word is your only way to claim God's promise to succeed.

markers you have, in the boxes below you can show three different you'd really like to be successful. Maybe it's in your math class or er field. Maybe you'd like to be a successful pianist or a great friend. **picture in each box.**

## SKG Puzzle Craze

### The Benefits of Meditation

Being *successful* is only one of God's promised outcomes for meditation. Let's look really hard at each verse we've been digging into. Using Joshua 1:8 and the verses from Psalm 119, find six words that describe the benefits of meditation. You'll use these to solve the crossword below.

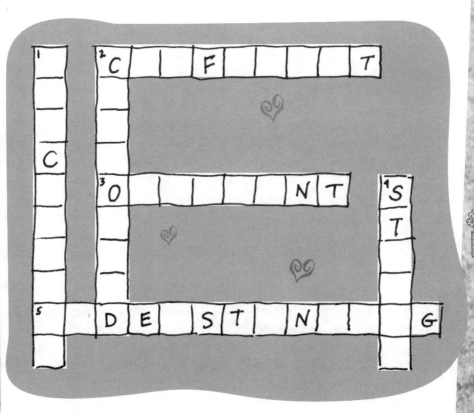

## Clues

Each word describes you. (Big hint: Like the word *successful!*)

DOWN

1. Joshua 1:8
2. Psalm 119:52
4. Psalm 119:117

ACROSS

2. Psalm 119:23
3. Psalm 119:48
5. Psalm 119:27

Answer on page 77

## Look Inside Yourself

After you "Dig In" by becoming a *studier* of the Bible, it's time to get ready to become a *pray-er*. I like to start by looking inside my own heart before I talk to God. This is kind of the bridge between studying and praying. When you see the "Look Inside" symbol, it means I'm getting ready to ask you some superpersonal questions. Ready?

**1** **Put a check mark next to each quality that is true of you. I am or feel . . .**

_____ SUCCESSFUL (with the things I do)

_____ CONFIDENT (enough to try new things and meet new people)

_____ OBEDIENT (to my parents, teachers, and God)

_____ STRONG (enough to keep going when I feel afraid)

_____ UNDERSTANDING (of God and others)

_____ COMFORTED (by God and my parents when things go wrong)

**2** **Fill in the blank, selecting one of the areas above where you hope God can change you.**

I wish I were more. . . . . . . . . . . . . . . . . . . . . . . . . . . . . . . . . . . . . . . . . . . . . .

**3** Now, here's the big one. How much time are you currently investing to meditate on God's Word each day? Remember, meditation includes studying the Bible *and* praying about what you have read! **Circle one.**

**A.** None

**B.** I spend some time reading or studying the Bible every day, but I don't pray very much. I need to pray more.

**C.** I pray every day, but I don't study the Bible very much. I need to start reading and studying regularly.

**D.** I spend a good amount of time both studying the Bible and praying. So, I am meditating. I'm not perfect, but I think I'm on track!

**4** What do you think you need to do based on what you've just studied while "digging in"?

### Reach up By Praying

When you see this graphic, you're going to add praying to your studying. I like to write my prayers down in a journal or diary. To help you learn how to do that, I'm going to help you write your prayers to God based on what we've just studied. First, fill in the blanks to personalize your prayer and then pray your prayer out loud.

Dear . . . . . . . . . . . . . . . . . . . . . (favorite name for God),

You are so. . . . . . . . . . . . . . . . . . . . . . . . . . . (your favorite descriptive word for God)! I praise You for who You are!

I need to ask You to forgive me because I realize that I'm not spending enough time . . . . . . . . . . . . . . . . . . . . . . . . . . . . . (studying Your Word or praying) and I want to do better.

I know that there are a lot of benefits to meditating every day. Today when I studied them, I realized that I wish I were more . . . . . . . . . . . . . . . . . . . . . . . . . . . . . . . . . . . . . . . . . . . . . . . . . . . . . . . . . . . . . .
I am really struggling in this area and this makes me feel. . . . . . . . . . . . . . . . . . . . . . . . . . . . . . . . . . . . . . . . . . . . Will You help me?

As I start this Secret Keeper Girl Bible study, I promise to meditate by studying the Bible and then praying. I look forward to what You'll do in me to change me.

I'm feeling very: . . . . . . . . excited . . . . . . . . overwhelmed

I give this emotion to You.

In Jesus' Name,

. . . . . . . . . . . . . . . . . . . . . . . . . . . . . . . . . . . . . . . . . . . . . . . . . . . . . . .
(SIGN HERE)

## Congratulations! You just meditated.

Now that you've practiced, we're ready to meditate on friendship and the greatest Friend ever. Welcome to *My Best Friend, Jesus!*

# How did Jesus pick friends for keeps?

O h, you just *hate* it when this happens! Your gym teacher has asked Trisha-the-All-Star and Julianne-the-Sure-to-Be-Soccer-Hero to pick teams for an all-girls game of kick ball. Code pink alert! This is *not* going to go well. You've been here before. Sure enough, Trisha starts by picking her BFF who's great at every sport. Julianne picks her total frenemy, a teammate who is sure to score. The slow, painful process of being the last one picked begins.

Relax! This is only a code pink *drill*. It's not the real thing! But does it sound familiar?

If it does, rest easy. You're not alone, and this Bible study is going to help you sort out stuff like that. There's an easy, highly tested, scientifically valid test to take to find out if you are going to have friendship problems in your life. I'd like you to take it now.

**Code Pink Quiz:**

*Are you a girl?*

Circle one. **Yes or No**

So, it's not really highly scientific. I was just joking about that. But it is fairly accurate. Let's check your results!

If you circled "yes" (and I hope you did since you're a Secret Keeper *Girl*), you are going to face challenges in friendship. Mean-girl moments, getting left out, the silent treatment, and a whole list of friendship challenges are just a given if you have girlish chemicals popping around in your body. Since those chemicals might have just gotten swirled around by the story about being left out, let's take a brain break and do an SKG Puzzle.

### SKG Puzzle Craze

Look at this drawing of four great friends from the Secret Keeper Girl fiction series. **Using the descriptions, try to figure out which girl is which.** I did the first one for you.

| | Danika is wearing a headband. | Kate is wearing glasses. | Toni is wearing a necklace without a drop. | Yuzi is wearing leggings. |
|---|---|---|---|---|
| **Yuzi** | no | | | |
| **Toni** | no | | | |
| **Danika** | YES! | | | |
| **Kate** | no | | | |

Even these fictional girls who love each other like crazy—run into friendship problems. You can't really avoid it, my Secret Keeper Girl.

So, what's a girl to do?

**Meditation Promise**
Remember, God promises us success when we meditate. So, if you meditate on what He says about friendship, you'll see some improvement in your friendships. I promise!

Well, let's look at the Best Friend a girl could ever have: Jesus. He is the ultimate friend and we can learn a lot about friendship by being His friend and becoming like Him. In this meditation session, we're going to try to meditate on the question: "How did Jesus pick friends for keeps?"

## Dig in By Studying

### John 15:9-17

In John 15, Jesus is talking to His closest friends—the twelve disciples—about how to be a good friend. And He says He has a way to measure true friendship. **Using your red marker, underline the verse that tells us how to do that.** (Hint: look for the word "measure")

**9** "I have loved you even as the Father has loved me. Remain in

my love. **10** When you obey me, you remain in my love, just as

I obey my Father and remain in his love. **11** I have told you this

so that you will be filled with my joy. Yes, your joy will over-

flow! **12** I command you to love each other in the same way that

I love you. **13** And here is how to measure it—the greatest love

is shown when people lay down their lives for their friends.

**14** You are my friends if you obey me. **15** I no longer call you servants, because a master doesn't confide in his servants. Now you are my friends, since I have told you everything the Father told me. **16** You didn't choose me. I chose you. I appointed you to go and produce fruit that will last, so that the Father will give you whatever you ask for, using my name.

**17** I command you to love each other."

Jesus said that the measure of true friendship is "people lay[ing] down their lives for their friends." No doubt, He was trying to tell them that He was about to die for them. Why?

The answer is in the most used word in the passage above. I don't think you'll have any trouble figuring out which word that is. Just look closely. **Using your red pen, put a big red heart around it each time it appears.**

**Fill in the blank.**
Jesus laid His life down for His friends because He . . . . . . . . . . . . . . . . . . . . . them.

## SKG Puzzle Craze

### Five things Jesus' disciples did to lay down their lives

OK, so *Jesus* loved His friends enough to die for them. That's something you probably already knew. You didn't have to dig too hard to find that. *But did you know that they did the same thing for Him?* Jesus' closest friends laid down their lives in many different ways. In this word search, you'll find five things they endured. **Find these words:**

## PRIS?N • LE?T ?A?ILIES • D??T? • L?FT J?B? • B??TI??S

```
A  B        N  B  R  I  N  O  T  I  G  T  I
P  E  E  E  E  I  E  O  S  B  G  N  P  I  N
R  E  L  A  R     S  I  L  M  I  S  T  A  F
I  E  E  P  T  I  L  E  F  T     J  O  B  S
S  O  F  O  R  I  F     A  L  G     L  I  E
O  N  T  P  E  I  N  E  I  I  A  F  E  R  I
O  E     L  O  P  B  G  S  I  S  A  N  H  E
N  S  J  F     E  I  D  A  E  T  H  T  H  S
T  J  O  A  S  J  D  E  A  T  L  A  F  B  S
   S  M  E  O     N  T  I  S  E  M  I  T  F
L  B  E  A  T  I  N  G  S  D  L  N  A  M  N
A  I  L  E  F  T     F  E  M  I  L  I  E  S
E  L  E  F  T     F  A  M  I  L  I  E  S  G
L  F  R  F  L  E  F  T     J  O  B  J  L  D
S  J  S  O  O  F  M  O  E  A  E  A  F  E
```

Answer on page 77

Each of the twelve disciples—Jesus' closest friends—left families and jobs. During Christ's life and after it, several of them left friends behind to travel to distant countries. They were often lonely. After Jesus died and came back to life, they were beaten and imprisoned, and many were killed in terrible ways.

If anyone has ever had friends who were keepers, He did. And I think one way you can have faithful friends is to begin friendships the same way that Jesus did.

Look again at John 15 on page 20. **Using your yellow pen, circle the two words in verse 16 that demonstrate how these friendships started.**

**Now, fill in the blank.**

Jesus' friends didn't . . . . . . . . . . . . . . Him. He . . . . . . . . . . . . . . them.

OK, hold that thought, while we look inside you!

## Look Inside Yourself

**1** Have you ever had any of the following happen to you? **Write yes or no beside each one.**

\_\_\_\_\_ You were the last one picked for a team.

\_\_\_\_\_ You felt left out because you weren't invited to a sleepover.

\_\_\_\_\_ No one sat by you at lunch. You sat alone.

\_\_\_\_\_ No one picked you to hang with after church.

When Jesus said, "I chose you" to His friends, He actually wasn't speaking English but Aramaic. He would have said "I eklegomia you." (Or something like that. It meant "I picked you.") Jesus' twelve friends on earth aren't His only friends. He meant these words for you and me, too. So, get this . . . Jesus picks you. Every time. Every day. He picks you, kid!

**2** How does that make you feel? **Using your colored markers, draw a picture of your emotion in the box on the next page.** Select colors that help you express your emotion.

**Under the *box*, name your picture descriptively.**

. . . . . . . . . . . . . . . . . . . . . . . . . . . . . . . . . . . . . . . . . . . . .

When I think of Jesus picking me as a friend, it makes me feel like I have butterflies in my tummy and confetti popping out of my ears! Whew! OK, come down from the high. (Boy, this lesson has been a roller-coaster ride for my heart!)

*Time out!* Our friendship with Jesus is nothing like our friendships with other girls. After all, He is GOD! We're not equal. He deserves and commands our respect, honor, and awe! But it's truly amazing to think that He . . . our Savior, our Lord, our God…desires for us to also to have a friendship with Him.

And, I really think that there is something for you and me to learn about our friendships with girls when we look at how Jesus started His friendship with the twelve disciples (and you and me). Let me see if I can get you there . . .

**3** **Circle one of the following to finish the sentence.**
When I am just getting started on a friendship, I tend to:

> **A.** Worry a lot about if the other girl likes me.
> I wait for her to approach me.

> **B.** I don't get too stressed, but I do put out feelers to see if I can gauge how she feels about me. I want her to like me as much as I think I like her. If she acts like she likes me, I might try to get something started.

> **C.** I look around to see who needs a friend.
> Then I choose to pursue her.

Did you select a totally, completely 100 percent honest answer? **OK, now underline the one that looks most like Jesus' example.**

I really think that most girls would have to honestly circle a or b when they describe how they pick friends. But clearly, Jesus' example is c. I really think that most of our friendships don't have much of a chance because rather than picking friends and focusing on their needs, we're all too focused on worrying about if someone is going to pick us! It's all wrong! It's completely backward from Jesus' example. Our friendships are bound to have problems until we fix this.

**4** What do you think you need to do based on what you've just studied while "digging in"? (We'll pray about it in just a moment!)

. . . . . . . . . . . . . . . . . . . . . . . . . . . . . . . . . . . . . . . . . . . . . . . . . . . . . . . . . . . .
. . . . . . . . . . . . . . . . . . . . . . . . . . . . . . . . . . . . . . . . . . . . . . . . . . . . . . . . . . . .
. . . . . . . . . . . . . . . . . . . . . . . . . . . . . . . . . . . . . . . . . . . . . . . . . . . . . . . . . . . .
. . . . . . . . . . . . . . . . . . . . . . . . . . . . . . . . . . . . . . . . . . . . . . . . . . . . . . . . . . . .

## Reach up To Talk to God

### Dear Jesus my Best Friend!

I really can't believe that You want to be my friend. Thanks for picking me! It makes me feel . . . . . . . . . . . . . . . . . . . . . . . when I think about it.

I need to ask You to forgive me. I've just realized that when I start a friendship I tend to . . . . . . . . . . . . . . . . . . . . . . . I know You want me to be more focused on the needs of others and not my own feelings. Help me to reorganize my mind and look for girls who need me to pick them.

Lord, right now, could You help me to think of someone who needs me to pick her?

(Pause and wait for God to talk to you. Just be still and patient!)

Wow, God! I thought of . . . . . . . . . . . . . . . . . . . . . . . . I really think she needs a friend because . . . . . . . . . . . . . . . . . . . . . . . . . . . . . . . . . . . . . . . . . . . . . . . . . . . . . . . . . . . . . . . . . . . . . . Could You help me to approach her?

In Jesus' Name,

(SIGN HERE)

# How did Jesus "do" friendship?

You are so not in the mood for excuses and lame apologies. It's the fifth time this afternoon that your little brother barged through your bedroom door. This time, he stepped on your school project and wrinkled the poster board when he jumped in wearing nothing but his Elmo boxers, a swim mask, and a Superman cape!

"Ahhhhhhhhhhhh!" you holler. "I . . . *you* . . . I can't believe . . . If you . . . !"

You search for words to describe your anger, but they don't come out. Suddenly, your BFF swoops in to save the day.

"Little Dude," she says, stepping between the two of you. "What she's trying to say is that she loves you a lot and likes to be near you, but right now we have to get this totally not-fun social science poster finished. In fact, we could get it done faster if you would cut out these pictures for us! Take them into your room and use your special scissors."

Little brother pushes his swim mask onto his head, grabs them with wide eyes, and marches off with his important assignment.

"When we're done, we should totally make brownies with him," says your Superhero BFF. You know she's just poured cool water on your steaming hot temper and rescued you from saying something you'd regret.

Suddenly you feel so much better!

Maybe your BFF has been taking a look at Jesus' friendships. It sure sounds like it. After Jesus picked His friends for keeps, He knew exactly how to "do" the friendship. He knew what came next. Today we're going to meditate on the question: "How did Jesus 'do' friendship?"

## Dig In By Studying
*Luke 10:38-42; John 11:1, 3, 5-8, 14, 17, 20-23, 28-29, 32-36, 39-44a*

Roll up your sleeves. Today you have *a lot* of Bible reading to do. (Remember this is a *Bible* study, after all!)

Jesus had more than just the twelve disciples for friends. Three of His other friends were especially close. They were Martha, Mary, and Lazarus—two sisters and a brother.

You've probably grown up reading their stories, but today we are going to look past the obvious parts of the story to really be friendship detectives. We're going to look for six things that Jesus did in this friendship that you can also do in your friendships. I've underlined the sentences that you need to analyze. In the balloon connected to it, I want you to write a contemporary version of what Jesus is doing by filling in the blanks.

> Jesus spent a lot of _____ with His friends.

**Luke 10:38** . . . Jesus and the disciples . . . came to a village where a woman named Martha welcomed them into her home. **39** Her sister, Mary, sat at the Lord's feet, listening to what he taught. **40** But Martha

> Jesus _____ them what He knew about life and God.

was worrying over the big dinner she was preparing. She came to Jesus and said, "Lord, doesn't it seem unfair to you that my sister just sits here while I do all the work? Tell her to come and help me."

**41** <u>But the Lord said to</u> <u>her, "My dear Martha, you</u> <u>are so upset over all these details!</u>

Jesus _____ His friends get along with each other

**42** There is really only one thing worth being concerned about. Mary has discovered it—and I won't take it away from her."

**John 11:1** A man named Lazarus was sick. He lived in Bethany with his sisters, Mary and Martha. **3** So the two sisters sent a message to Jesus telling him, "Lord, the one you love is very sick." **5** Although Jesus loved Martha, Mary, and Lazarus, **6** he stayed where he was for the next two days and did not go to them. **7** Finally after two days, he said to his disciples, "Let's go to Judea

Jesus _____ His own life to help them

again." **8** <u>But his disciples</u> <u>objected. Teacher," they said, "only</u> <u>a few days ago the Jewish leaders in</u> <u>Judea were trying to kill you. Are you going there again?"</u>

**14** Then he told them plainly, "Lazarus is dead." **17** When Jesus arrived at Bethany, he was told that Lazarus had already been in his grave for four days. **20** When Martha got word that Jesus was coming, she went to meet him. But Mary stayed at home. **21** Martha said to Jesus, "Lord, if you had been here, my brother would not have died. **22** But even now I know that God will give you whatever you ask." **23** Jesus told her, "Your brother will rise again." **28** Then she left him and returned to Mary. She called Mary aside from the mourners and told her, "The Teacher is here and wants to see you." **29** So Mary immediately went to him. **32** When Mary arrived and saw Jesus, she fell down at his feet and said, "Lord, if you had been here, my brother would not have died." **33** When Jesus saw her weeping and saw the other people wailing with her, he was moved with indignation and was deeply troubled. **34** "Where have you put him?" he asked them. They told him, "Lord, come and see."

**35** Then Jesus wept.

**36** The people who were standing nearby said, "See how much he loved him." **39** "Roll the stone aside,"

Jesus _____ with and for His friends.

Jesus told them. But Martha, the dead man's sister, said, "Lord, by now the smell will be terrible because he has been dead for four days."

**40** Jesus responded, "Didn't I tell you that you will see God's glory if you believe?" **41** So they rolled the stone aside. Then Jesus looked up to heaven and said, "Father, thank you for hearing me. **42** You always hear me, but I said it out loud for the sake of all these people standing here, so they will believe you sent me." **43** Then Jesus shouted, "Lazarus, come out!"

**44** And Lazarus came out.

Jesus _____ for His friends.

Answers on page 77

**What are the six things you and I can do?** The list might look like this. See if you can fill in the blanks.

**1.** Spend a lot of . . . . . . . . . . . . . . . . . . . . . . with friends.

**2.** . . . . . . . . . . . . . . . . . . . . . them what you know about life and God.

**3.** Help my friends. . . . . . . . . . . . . . . . . . . . . with each other.

**4.** Take time to. . . . . . . . . . . . . . . . . . . . .them.

**5.** . . . . . . . . . . . . . . . . . . . . . with and for them.

**6.** . . . . . . . . . . . . . . . . . . . . .for them.

**SKG Puzzle Craze**

*Why did Jesus "do" friendship the way He did?*

SJUES VLODE ATHRMA, YMRA, DAN ZARSULA!

. . . . . . . . . . . . . .    . . . . . . . . . . . . . . .    . . . . . . . . . . . . ,    . . . . . . . . . . . . . ,

. . . . . . . . . . . . . . . . . . . . . . . . . . . . ! —John 11:5

That takes us back to our first meditation when we looked at why Jesus picked friends for keeps. He loved them. He picked His friends (including you) because of love. And, He does friendship the way He does out of love!

He is not only our greatest friend, but since He is perfect, He models great friendship for us. Speaking of which, let's take a look inside you!

Answer on page 77

## Look Inside Yourself

**1 Using *all* your markers, draw a picture of you and your BFF in the *box below*.** If you have a great photo, you can just paste it there.

**2** Let's see if you're modeling Jesus' example of friendship with her.
**Check the appropriate box.**

| | Totally! Got it covered! | Oops! I don't do this! | Hmm? Could do better. |
|---|---|---|---|
| I teach her what I know about life and God. | ✓ | | |
| I spend a lot of time with her. | | | ✓ |
| I get in the middle of her fights to solve them. | ✓ | | |
| I take risks to help her. | | | |
| I cry with and for her. | | | |
| I pray for her. | | ✓ | |

**3** Based on your responses, **write two goals** that will help you to be more like Jesus in the way you "do" friendship with your BFF.

**GOAL #1** ......................................................

..............................................................

..............................................................

..............................................................

**GOAL #2** . . . . . . . . . . . . . . . . . . . . . . . . . . . . . . . . . . . . . . . . . . . .

. . . . . . . . . . . . . . . . . . . . . . . . . . . . . . . . . . . . . . . . . . . . . . . . . . . . . . . . .

. . . . . . . . . . . . . . . . . . . . . . . . . . . . . . . . . . . . . . . . . . . . . . . . . . . . . . . . .

. . . . . . . . . . . . . . . . . . . . . . . . . . . . . . . . . . . . . . . . . . . . . . . . . . . . . . . .

❧ ❧ ❧

## Reach up To Talk to God

### Dear Jesus:

What a great friend You are! I never really saw all of those things
You did to be a great friend to Martha, Mary, and Lazarus. Those
are good ideas for me in my friendships. I was especially amazed
to learn that You . . . . . . . . . . . . . . . . . . . . . . . . . . . . . . . . . . . . . . . . . . .

My best friend is . . . . . . . . . . . . . . . . . . . . . . . . . . , but You already know that.
Two goals I have are to . . . . . . . . . . . . . . . . . . . . . . . . . . . . . . . . . . . . . . . . .
and to . . . . . . . . . . . . . . . . . . . . . . . . . . . . . . . . . . . . . . . . . . . . . . . . . . . . . .
Give me a heart to do this.

In Jesus' Name,

. . . . . . . . . . . . . . . . . . . . . . . . . . . . . . . . . . . . . . . . . . . . . . . . . . . . . .
(SIGN HERE)

❧ ❧ ❧

34

# What did Jesus do when His friends got jealous?

I t's Monday at lunch and things aren't going too well. None of your friends are acting right. It all started when you walked out of homeroom with Miss New Girl. Your BFF looked at you like you had slapped her. You were just trying to be nice! Now, she's sitting with someone else and that someone else's BFF at lunch. You hear them whispering over their PB&J.

Wait! Did you just hear your name? Maybe they're going to invite you over. Nope! They're laughing now. Is it possible that they're laughing *at* you? An internal girls-only alarm system goes off in your heart. It's a BFF takeover . . . a three-friend gang up!

Easy now . . . breathe!

Do your friends ever get jealous? Do you?

Guess what? So did Jesus' friends. James and John were two of Jesus' closest friends. (Only Peter enjoyed as close a friendship.) But once, those two best buddies almost caused a complete friendship meltdown in the inner circle of Jesus' twelve closest friends. Today we're going to meditate on the question, "What did Jesus do when His friends got jealous?"

## Dig in By Studying
### Matthew 20:20-28

It all started when James and John's mama arrived on the scene. She apparently had noticed that Jesus was especially close to her boys. Maybe she also knew that Jesus liked Peter a lot. Perhaps she grew jealous. But the bottom line is that she got a crazy idea and headed out to ask Jesus what He thought about it. **Underline her idea on the next page using your green-with-envy marker.**

**20** Then the mother of James and John, the sons of Zebedee, came to Jesus with her sons. She knelt respectfully to ask a favor. **21** "What is your request?" he asked. She replied, "In your Kingdom, will you let my two sons sit in places of honor next to you, one at your right and the other at your left?"... **23** [Jesus said,] "But I have no right to say who will sit on the thrones next to mine. My Father has prepared those places for the ones he has chosen." **24** When the ten other disciples heard what James and John had asked, they were indignant. **25** But Jesus called them together and said, "You know that in this world kings are tyrants, and officials lord it over the people beneath them. **26** But among you it should be quite different. Whoever wants to be a leader among you must be your servant, **27** and whoever wants to be first must become your slave. **28** For even I, the Son of Man, came here not to be served but to serve others, and to give my life as a ransom for many."

You should have underlined "In your Kingdom, will you let my two sons sit in places of honor next to you, one at your right and the other at your left?" Basically Mom decides that James and John deserve to be in the two closest positions of honor to Jesus. But did she come to that all on her own? Nope. She was just the designated spokesperson.

**Read verse 20 and use your green-with-envy marker to circle the three words that tell you who came to Jesus with her.**

Seems like James and John had a little something to do with this plot to rule the kingdom of God. They'd made a plan that left everyone else out and created a really nasty emotion in the other disciples.

**Read verse 24. Put a green-with-envy box around the word that describes how the other ten disciples felt.**

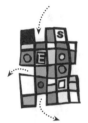

## SKG Puzzle Craze
*Some other words for indignant*

Indignant. That's how the other ten disciples felt when they found out James and John had sought out this special honor. *They disrupted the careful balance of friendship in their little group by weighing their own value against the others.* There are six words in the word search below that describe what it means to feel indignant. **Start with the first letter, A, and cross out every other one to find six words that describe "Indignant."**

AIZNTSGUVLRTQETDXMRASDVICNVFRUWRSIDARTTEWDM

RREKSHEYNUTIFRUWLEJFEGAQLJOBUCSEOUFIFEEHNKDZEED

1.\_\_\_ \_\_\_ \_\_\_ \_\_\_ \_\_\_ \_\_\_ \_\_\_ \_\_\_    2.\_\_\_ \_\_\_ \_\_\_

3.\_\_\_ \_\_\_ \_\_\_ \_\_\_ \_\_\_ \_\_\_ \_\_\_ \_\_\_ \_\_\_ \_\_\_

4.\_\_\_ \_\_\_ \_\_\_ \_\_\_ \_\_\_ \_\_\_ \_\_\_ \_\_\_ \_\_\_

5.\_\_\_ \_\_\_ \_\_\_ \_\_\_ \_\_\_ \_\_\_ \_\_\_

6.\_\_\_ \_\_\_ \_\_\_ \_\_\_ \_\_\_ \_\_\_ \_\_\_ \_\_\_

Bible scholars (older dudes who study the Bible like crazy) say that what happened with the disciples was pretty ugly. It included nasty gestures like giving James and John dirty looks or turning their backs to them. It also included angry words that probably grew to crazed yelling. James and John never should have tried to make themselves to be of more value. It only added

Answer on page 77

jealousy to their side of the scale, and things got so out of control that it looked a lot more like mean-girl chaos than the meeting of God's twelve choice followers.

Speaking of which, let's take a look inside you!

## Look Inside Yourself

Even though jealousy is a sin we have all committed, most of us don't like to admit we struggle with it (or create it). We end up "weighing" ourselves against each other when we make comparisons or competing, like James and John did.

**1** **First write your name in the *left label* of the scale below.** Write your BFF's name on the center label. Now, think of the name of someone who is also your BFF's friend but not really yours. Write her name on the right label of the scale.

YOUR NAME

BFF'S FRIEND'S NAME

YOUR BFF'S NAME

**2** Read the phrases *below* and put an *"x"* beside any of the ones you have thought when you think about your BFF's other friend.

_____ "I wonder who my BFF likes better." (**sad**)

_____ "But I've known my BFF longer than she has!"

_____ "I wonder if she is more fun than I am?"

_____ "I'm just not going to be friends with either of them!"

_____ "Am I losing my BFF?"

Now, using only the ones you've checked, write a word beside it that describes how you feel when you think that thought. I did the first one so you have an example. If I thought, "I wonder who my BFF likes better," it would make me sad.

**Take those words and write them on the scale above your name.**

**3** What happens to the delicate balance of friendship when you weigh your value against another person's? **Circle one:**

**A.** Nothing, life is great and we all get to eat Nerds.

**B.** The "other girl" gets weighed down by my ugly feelings.

**C.** My best friend feels stuck in the middle.

**D.** I get weighed down by my ugly feelings.

Not only does your BFF feel torn, but you get to carry the heavy weight of those ugly emotions created by jealousy. Not your friend. Not your friend's other friend. You. You get to carry the ugly emotions around.

**4** Jesus' approach to jealousy was unlike ours. He basically said, "Hey, kings were created to fight battles, but you guys were created to be friends. Friends don't do this. They serve each other. Even I came to serve." Seems like the best solution to a jealousy triangle is to do something to serve the person you're jealous of. What is something nice that you can do for your BFF's other friend? Using the "How-can-I-serve-you?" chatter box below, write some ideas in the triangles for how you can serve your BFF's other friend. I got you started with a few ideas. After you write these ideas, follow the directions to create your chatter box!

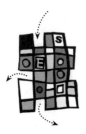

## SKG Puzzle Craze
### The "How-can-I-serve-you" Chatter Box

After you write in your ideas for serving, use these directions to fold your Chatter Box and use it.

**1.** Cut out the big square. Fold and unfold it in half diagonally in both directions to make an X. Place the square picture side down.

**2.** Fold each corner to point into the center.

**3.** Flip so that the flaps are facedown. Then fold each corner to the center.

**4.** Fold in half this way to crease.

**5.** Then unfold and fold in half the other way.

**6.** Stick both thumbs and pointer fingers into the four pockets. Push all the pockets to a point to begin playing.

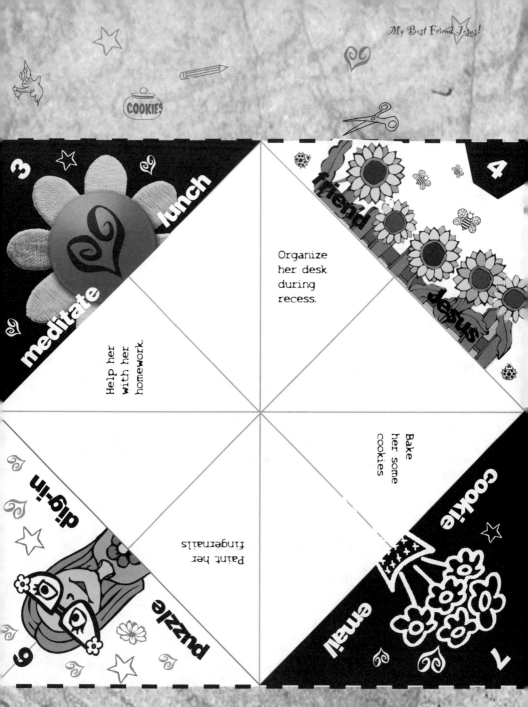

3

lunch

meditate

Organize
her desk
during
recess.

friend

4

Jesus

Help her
with her
homework.

Bake
her some
cookies

dig-in

cookie

Paint her
fingernails

email

puzzle

6

7

SKG Chatter-Box!

## TO PLAY CHATTER-BOX:

Take your chatter box to school or church and ask your BFF to use it to help you pick something neat you can do for her friend . . . who may be about to become yours!

**1.** Insert your fingers and thumbs under the numbered flaps on the chatter box.

**2.** Ask your BFF's friend to choose a number from one of the outside flaps, or choose one yourself. Open and close your fingers that number of times, moving your fingers from front to back and then sideways.

**3.** Have your friend choose one of the words on the inside of the chatter box. Spell out the word, opening and closing your fingers with each letter.

**4.** Ask your friend to pick one of the words that shows. Open that flap and read what you get to do to serve her. And do it!

## Reach up To Talk to God

*Dear Jesus:*

Wow! I can't believe that even Your closest friends struggled with jealousy. When I think about this I have to say. . . . . . . . . . .

. . . . . . . . . . . . . . . . . . . . . . . . . . . . . . . . . . . . . . . . . . . . . . . . . . . . . . . . . .

. . . . . . . . . . . . . . . . . . . . . . . . . . . . . . . . . . . . . . . . . . . . . . . . . . . . . . . . . .

God, I'm really struggling a little bit myself. Here's what You need to know about it. . . . . . . . . . . . . . . . . . . . . . . . . . . . . . . . . . . . . . . . . . . . . . . . . . . . .

. . . . . . . . . . . . . . . . . . . . . . . . . . . . . . . . . . . . . . . . . . . . . . . . . . . . . . . . . .

. . . . . . . . . . . . . . . . . . . . . . . . . . . . . . . . . . . . . . . . . . . . . . . . . . . . . . . . . .

When I wrote the ideas of how I can serve this person, it made me feel . . . . . . . . . . .

. . . . . . . . . . . . . . . . . . . . . . . . . . . . . . . . . . . . . . . . . . . . . . . . . . . . . . . . . .

. . . . . . . . . . . . . . . . . . . . . . . . . . . . . . . . . . . . . . . . . . . . . . . . . . . . . . . . . .

Please open up doors for me to serve her and help my BFF to understand how much I need her help.

In Jesus' Name,

. . . . . . . . . . . . . . . . . . . . . . . . . . . . . . . . . . . . . . . . . . . . . . . . . . . . . . . . . .

(SIGN HERE)

# What did Jesus do when His friends hurt Him?

## Check out this terrible scene!

**Y**ou walk into the bathroom at church and you hear two voices chattering. You immediately recognize one of them as your good friend. You're just about to pipe up and say "hi" when the voice you don't recognize says something that could make the rays of the sun freeze!

"I hear [insert your name here] is totally annoying. Do you know her?" The words echo off the metal bathroom doors and pierce your heart. Silence follows.

"Uh, no," you hear your friend say. "I don't know her . . . much."

You slink out of the bathroom with tears burning your eyes. What should you do next?

Well, how about we take a look at what Jesus did! If James and John were two of His closest friends, the only other was Peter. Guess what Peter did? He denied he was friends with Jesus. Today, we're going to meditate on the question: "What did Jesus do when His friends hurt Him?"

### Dig in By Studying
*John 18:15-17, 25-27*

Peter denied he was Jesus' friend. Look at the passage below to find out how many times Peter did this. **Use your I'm-so-blue marker to circle each incident.**

**15** Simon Peter followed along behind, as did another of the disciples. That other disciple was acquainted with the high priest, so he was allowed to enter the courtyard with Jesus. **16** Peter stood outside the gate. Then the other disciple spoke to the woman watching at the gate, and she let Peter in. **17** The woman asked Peter, "Aren't you one of Jesus' disciples?" "No," he said, "I am not." **25** Meanwhile, as Simon Peter was standing by the fire, they asked him again, "Aren't you one of his disciples?" "I am not," he said. **26** But one of the household servants of the high priest, a relative of the man whose ear Peter had cut off, asked, "Didn't I see you out there in the olive grove with Jesus?" **27** Again Peter denied it. And immediately a rooster crowed.

How many times did Peter say he wasn't Jesus' friend? **Write the answer on the line below.**

. . . . . . . . . . . . . . . . . . . . . . . . . . . . . . . . . . . . . . . . . . . . . . . . . . . . .

Dude! That must have hurt bad. I don't know about you, but I'd have had a massive cry fest! This was one of Jesus' three closest friends and he said he wasn't Jesus' friend THREE times! What did Jesus do? Let's check it out. But first, a quick timeline.

## SKG Puzzle Craze

*Create a timeline of Jesus and Peter's friendship crisis*

Using the line below, add in the proper order these important events that happened between the time that Peter denied Jesus and the time that Jesus caught up with him for their first interaction. **Draw pictures to symbolize these three events, taking care to unscramble the order!**

• Jesus is buried in a tomb

• Jesus dies on the cross

• Jesus rises from the dead

*1*  *2*  *3*  *4*  *5*

Peter

Denies

Jesus

draw

pictures

here

Jesus

Meets

Peter

Answer on page 77

Now, read the exciting first interaction between Jesus and Peter. It's the first time they've had one-on-one interaction since Peter has said three times that he was not Jesus' friend. I find four things that Jesus does for Peter. See if you can find them. Let's put away that "I'm-so-blue" marker and trade it for a happy sunshine yellow. **Circle four things that Jesus does for Peter.**

## John 21:1–13, 15, 19

**1** Later Jesus appeared again to the disciples beside the Sea of Galilee. This is how it happened. **2** Several of the disciples were there— [including] Simon Peter . . . **3** Simon Peter said, "I'm going fishing." "We'll come, too," they all said. So they went out in the boat, but they caught nothing all night. **4** At dawn the disciples saw Jesus standing on the beach, but they couldn't see who he was. **5** He called out, "Friends, have you caught any fish?" "No," they replied. **6** Then he said, "Throw out your net on the right-hand side of the boat, and you'll get plenty of fish!" So they did, and they couldn't draw in the net because there were so many fish in it. **7** Then the disciple whom Jesus loved said to Peter, "It is the Lord!" When Simon Peter heard that it was the Lord, he . . . jumped into the water, and swam ashore. **9** When [he] got there, [he] saw that a charcoal fire was burning and fish were frying over it, and there was bread.

**10** "Bring some of the fish you've just caught," Jesus said. **11** So Simon Peter

went aboard and dragged the net to the shore. There were 153 large fish,

and yet the net hadn't torn. **12** "Now come and have some breakfast!"

Jesus said. . . . **13** Then Jesus served them the bread and the fish.

**15** After breakfast Jesus said to Simon Peter, "Simon son of John, do you

love me more than these?" "Yes, Lord," Peter replied, "you know I love you."

**. . . 19 . . .** Then Jesus told him, "Follow me."

Jesus helped Peter and the others catch an enormous load of fish. He built Peter a nice, cozy campfire to cuddle up next to. He served him breakfast. And He invited him to follow Him—to once again be His friend. In fact, Jesus made Peter a leader of the church and called him "the Rock!"

Is that what you would have done? Let's look inside.

## Look Inside Yourself

**1** Have any of these things ever happened to you?
**Put an "x" beside any that have.**

_____ You invite a friend over and she says she has to stay home, but then you find out she accepted an invitation to another girl's house.

_____ You tell your friend a secret, and then you find out that she told everyone else.

_____ You catch two of your friends laughing at you when something bad happens.

_____ Miss Born-to-Be-Mean blames you for losing the soccer game *in front of everyone*. Your BFF doesn't defend you.

_____ You buy a shirt you really like. You told your friend you were going to buy it. She goes out and buys the same one even though she knows you don't like it when she does that.

_____ (Add your own here.). . . . . . . . . . . . . . . . . . . . . . . . . . . . . . . . . . . . .
. . . . . . . . . . . . . . . . . . . . . . . . . . . . . . . . . . . . . . . . . . . . . . . . . . . . . . .
. . . . . . . . . . . . . . . . . . . . . . . . . . . . . . . . . . . . . . . . . . . . . . . . . . . . . . .
. . . . . . . . . . . . . . . . . . . . . . . . . . . . . . . . . . . . . . . . . . . . . . . . . . . . . . .

**2** What did you do? **Circle all that apply.**

# Cried

## Told other friends not to trust that girl

**Promised I'd never be friends with her again** *

*Gave her time to say she was sorry, and she did*

Wrote her a long email asking if everything was cool

Baked her our fav snack and took it to her.

*

**STOMPED OFF AND FOUND A NEW FRIEND TO REPLACE HER**

**Made her a cozy campfire**

**Wrote her a long email telling her to forget it!**

*

\* Look at what you just circled above. Are these things Jesus would have done?

**3** Write a list of four things you can do the next time your friend hurts you, based on Jesus' example.

**Jesus' List of To-Do's**
For a Friend Who Hurt Him

**1.** Create miraculous catch of fish!

**2.** Start a roaring campfire!

**3.** Serve a yummy breakfast!

**4.** Ask friend to be friends again!

**My List of To-Do's**
For a Friend Who Hurts Me

**1.** . . . . . . . . . . . . . . . . . . . . . . . . . . . .

. . . . . . . . . . . . . . . . . . . . . . . . . . . .

**2.** . . . . . . . . . . . . . . . . . . . . . . . . . . .

. . . . . . . . . . . . . . . . . . . . . . . . . . . .

**3.** . . . . . . . . . . . . . . . . . . . . . . . . . . . .

. . . . . . . . . . . . . . . . . . . . . . . . . . . .

**4.** . . . . . . . . . . . . . . . . . . . . . . . . . . .

. . . . . . . . . . . . . . . . . . . . . . . . . . . .

### Reach up To Talk to God
## Dear Best Friend, Jesus:

It must have really hurt when Peter said he wasn't Your friend. I imagine that when You found out You probably . . . . . . . . . . .
. . . . . . . . . . . . . . . . . . . . . . . . . . . . . . . . . . . . . . .

I've been hurt by friends too. Only I didn't react the same way You did. Instead, I . . . . . . . . . . . . . . . . . . . . . . . . . . . .and I . . . . . . . . . . . . . . . . . . . . . . . . . . .

From now on, I intend to respond like You did. Help me to do this. I know it won't be easy.

In Jesus' Name,

. . . . . . . . . . . . . . . . . . . . . . . . . . . . . . . . . . . . . . .
(SIGN HERE)

# How can I be a good friend to Jesus?

chool was tough today. One uber-math test plus one essay equals need for a break this afternoon. You hit the kitchen first for a tall glass of milk and some cookies, then you escape to your bedroom for some serious refueling. But Mom has different plans.

"(Insert your name here), could you come wash the dishes for me? I'm running behind," she calls just as you're about to flop onto your bed with a good book. Something inside of you boils, and you want to grumble. Then you think better and decide you won't grumble, you'll just *explain* why you can't do it. But you quickly come to your senses and drag yourself downstairs, where you are greeted by a tower of soap bubbles that you're certain could top Mt. Everest. You just hope the dishes aren't stacked that high.

You dive in to the task while your mom is folding laundry behind you. Making an intentional effort to be obedient seems to have opened the door of your heart . . . and your mom's! Before you know it, you and your mom are laughing and talking together. You are enjoying *friendship* with your mom.

I hope this story helps you take a look at an even more unique friendship—friendship with Jesus! Today we're going to meditate on the question, "How can I be a good friend to Jesus?"

## Dig In By Studying
### John 15:9-17

This is going to sound really familiar. It's the passage we started with. (Remember, it brought us the exciting news that Jesus "picked" us to be friends!) Why? Because Jesus clearly tells us how we can be His friend.

**Using a rainbow of colors, draw a rainbow over the four words that tell us what we must do to be Jesus' friend. Hint: It begins, "You are my friends . . . "**

**9** "I have loved you even as the Father has loved me. Remain in my love.

**10** When you obey me, you remain in my love, just as I obey my Father

and remain in his love. **11** I have told you this so that you will be filled

with my joy. Yes, your joy will overflow! **12** I command you to love each

other in the same way that I love you. **13** And here is how to measure

it—the greatest love is shown when people lay down their lives for

their friends. **14** You are my friends if you obey me. **15** I no longer

call you servants, because a master doesn't confide in his servants. Now

you are my friends, since I have told you everything the Father told

me. **16** You didn't choose me. I chose you. I appointed you to go and

produce fruit that will last, so that the Father will give you whatever

you ask for, using my name. **17** I command you to love each other."

What does Jesus want us to do? **Write it on the line below.**

......................................................................

He said that one of the ways we show that we are His friends is by obeying Him. That's kind of like what happens when you obey your mom. In obeying her, you produce something. What?

**Read verse 16 above and circle the word that tells us what our obedience produces. Fill in the blanks.**

Obeying Jesus produces ...............................................
that will ...........................................................
......................................................................

## SKG Puzzle Craze

### What kind of fruit was Jesus talking about?

Was Jesus talking about the brown, wrinkly fruit that grows in the Middle East (where He lived) called a date? Ew! Yuck. Of course not! **Complete the crossword puzzle by selecting the kind of fruit that you think Jesus was talking about in John 15.**

## Clues:

Each word is one of the . . . . . . . . . . . . . . . . . . . . . . . . of the Spirit.

ACROSS
3. A bouncy bundle of joy or a little orange kumquat.
4. Some kindness or a tart little star fruit.
5. Peace that passes understanding or a kiwi.
6. Some serious self-control or a guava from Mexico.

DOWN
1. A dose of goodness or a bowl of Chinese lychee.
2. Gentleness or a sweet honeydew melon.
7. A bunch of love or a big juicy watermelon.

55

Answers on page 77

The fruit of obedience that Jesus was talking about wasn't Chinese lychee, was it? It was fruit like love, joy, peace, patience, kindness, gentleness, goodness, faithfulness, and self-control.

What fruit from the list above do you think that you would produce if you did the dishes for your mom when she asked even though you were totally worn out? **Write your idea below:**

. . . . . . . . . . . . . . . . . . . . . . . . . . . . . . . . . . . . . . . . . . . . . . . . . . . . . . . . . .

Maybe you wrote self-control. That would be a good choice. (But any of them might be, so no answer is wrong.) I would say self-control because you didn't express your frustration and exhaustion. You sure could have freaked on her, but you didn't. You were self-controlled. You obeyed, and that produced *self-control,* which produced *peace,* which made your *joy* even greater. And that sets the stage for you to interact not only as mother and daughter but as friends.

How is this a lot like what happens when we obey Jesus? To find out, let's take a look inside of you!

## Look Inside Yourself

Think of something that Jesus told you to do, *but you did not obey.* (Some ideas might include inviting the new girl to sit with you, taking out the trash when your mom told you to, or telling a friend you were sorry for something you did.) **In the boxes that follow, draw a four-scene cartoon dramatization.**

**2** What "fruit" came out of that experience? Circle all that apply.

Sadness * Broken Friendship Crying

Lying

Loneliness

Discipline ANGER *

* Guilt Loss of privilege
(like allowance)

Just like our moms or dads have to move into the role of discipliner (to take away privileges like allowance or free time) or teacher (as they teach us to respond differently) when we disobey them, Jesus has to do the same. Why? He loves us! They also might have to be busy being our comforter (when we cry). The role they are forced to operate in when you disobey is not that of friend, is it? **Circle one.**

YES NO

**3** Now, think of a time when you clearly obeyed Jesus. (Ideas might include turning off the TV to go help your mom set the table, giving up an afternoon to go visit your sick grandma, or getting up early to read your Bible.) **Using the cartoon strip *below*, draw a picture of that story.**

**4** Using your list of fruit from the crossword puzzle, which ones did you experience as a result of obeying? Write them below.

. . . . . . . . . . . . . . . . . . . . . . . . . . . . . . . . . . . . . . . . . . . . . . . . . .

. . . . . . . . . . . . . . . . . . . . . . . . . . . . . . . . . . . . . . . . . . . . . . . . . .

Obedience created that fruit in your life! It also opened the door for you to be Jesus' friend. It's not that Jesus doesn't want to be your friend when you disobey. But, just like with your mom and dad, your obedience opens the door for laughter, fellowship, and friendship. Can you understand how that works now? Good! Let's pray about it.

## Reach up To Talk to God

### Dear Jesus:

**I really do want to be Your friend. I:**

_____ never knew that I needed to obey You to be Your friend.

_____ already knew that I needed to obey You to be Your friend.

**In thinking about it today, I know that:**

_____ I need to work on this. I'm not very obedient.

_____ I need to be more consistent. I obey sometimes, but not always.

_____ I'm trying. I think I'm usually obedient.

Of course, we all need a little help in some area. I need help . . . . . . . . . . . . . . . . .
. . . . . . . . . . . . . . . . . . . . . . . . . . . . . . . . . . . . . . . . . . . . . . . . . . . . . . . . . . . . . . . .
. . . . . . . . . . . . . . . . . . . . . . . . . . . . . . . . . . . . . . . . . . . . . . . . . . . . . . . . . . . . . . . .

As a matter of a fact, right now when I pray about being obedient, I find myself thinking that I need to . . . . . . . . . . . . . . . . . . . . . . . . . . . . . . . . . . . . . . . . . . . . . . . .
I'm going to get started on that right away.

In Jesus' Name,

. . . . . . . . . . . . . . . . . . . . . . . . . . . . . . . . . . . . . . . . . . . . . . . . . . . . . . . . . . . . .
(SIGN HERE)

# Who needs to meet my friend Jesus?

I t's only the first week of summer and you've already turned your hair green from the chlorine in the pool, pulled enough weeds from your mom's flower bed to fill a small state, and given your dog six bubble baths. Now, you're bored.

But today, you made a fabulous new friend at church. And just in time.

The new girl? She's practically your emotional twin. She loves dogs. So do you. She loves chocolate chip ice cream. So do you. She's totally into Nick at Nite. So are you. She's in dance. So are you. It's like she was made to be your friend.

You race up to your mom with her. Jumping up and down like you're on an invisible pogo stick, you ask, "Mom! Can we have a sleepover? Pleeeease!"

When we find a new friend, we just can't wait to show the person off. We act a little insane sometimes. Are you ever a little insane about sharing your friendship with Jesus? In this meditation we'll explore the question, "Who needs to meet my friend Jesus?"

### Dig in By Studying
Luke 12:4, 6:-8; John 17:20; Romans 8:34; Hebrews 7:25

Before we look at who needs to meet your friend Jesus, let's take a minute to remember who picked whom to be friends. Fill in the blanks.

I didn't . . . . . . . . . . . . . . . . . . . . . . . . Jesus. He . . . . . . . . . . . . . . . . . . . . . . . . me!

Jesus picked you! Why? *Because He loves you.*

I remember the day that Jesus "picked" me. I was only four and a half. (If I really think hard about it and look in my Bible, I realize that Jesus "picked me" before the world was created! Whoa!) But it was on that day that I decided to respond and to ask Him to live in my heart. Have you done that? Oh, I hope so! **If you have, write the story of that day in the space below:**

. . . . . . . . . . . . . . . . . . . . . . . . . . . . . . . . . . . . . . . . . . . . . . . . . . . . . . . . . .

. . . . . . . . . . . . . . . . . . . . . . . . . . . . . . . . . . . . . . . . . . . . . . . . . . . . . . . . . .

. . . . . . . . . . . . . . . . . . . . . . . . . . . . . . . . . . . . . . . . . . . . . . . . . . . . . . . . . .

. . . . . . . . . . . . . . . . . . . . . . . . . . . . . . . . . . . . . . . . . . . . . . . . . . . . . . . . . .

. . . . . . . . . . . . . . . . . . . . . . . . . . . . . . . . . . . . . . . . . . . . . . . . . . . . . . . . . .

. . . . . . . . . . . . . . . . . . . . . . . . . . . . . . . . . . . . . . . . . . . . . . . . . . . . . . . . . .

. . . . . . . . . . . . . . . . . . . . . . . . . . . . . . . . . . . . . . . . . . . . . . . . . . . . . . . . . .

. . . . . . . . . . . . . . . . . . . . . . . . . . . . . . . . . . . . . . . . . . . . . . . . . . . . . . . . . .

. . . . . . . . . . . . . . . . . . . . . . . . . . . . . . . . . . . . . . . . . . . . . . . . . . . . . . . . . .

. . . . . . . . . . . . . . . . . . . . . . . . . . . . . . . . . . . . . . . . . . . . . . . . . . . . . . . . . .

If you haven't, turn to page 75 to hear my whole story! After you read it, come back to this page! I'll be waiting!

OK, did you write your story or read mine? If you read mine, maybe you prayed to ask Jesus to live in your heart too! Guess what? You get to go back and write about it above.

Stop!

I hope you've made that decision to follow Jesus. I hope you love Him because He sure does love you! Just how much? Check it out. **Circle the greeting Jesus uses below.**

### Luke 12:4, 6–8

"Dear friends . . . **6** what is the price of five sparrows?

A couple of pennies? Yet God does not forget a single one of them.

**7** And the very hairs on your head are all numbered. So don't be afraid;

you are more valuable to him than a whole flock of sparrows.

**8** And I assure you of this: If anyone acknowledges me publicly here

on earth, I, the Son of Man, will openly acknowledge that person in

the presence of God's angels."

Right off the bat, He calls us friends! Cool, huh?

Now, find the two things in verse 6 that Jesus says He values to the point of never forgetting. **Using any markers you want, draw a picture of each of them directly above the word.**

Jesus says He will never forget even the tiniest of sparrows or a penny of little worth. And then He says that He even has something on you numbered. What? **Write it below.**

. . . . . . . . . . . . . . . . . . . . . . . . . . . . . . . . . . . . . . . . . . . . . . . . . . . . . . . . . . . . . .

Why don't you just grab a little bunch of your hair and try to count it. Go ahead. **Circle your estimate of how many hairs you have *below*.**

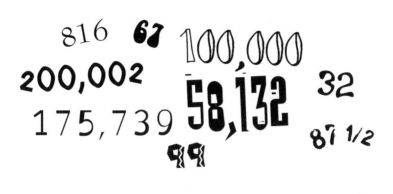

816  67  100,000

200,002  58,132  32

175,739  87 1/2

99

Did you guess 100,000? You're probably close. It varies based on a lot of factors, including hair color.

Based on hair color and estimates, the Secret Keeper Girl fiction characters have this many hairs on their heads:

People with black hair have about 108,000.

People with brown hair have about 100,000.

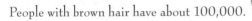

People with blonde hair have about 140,000.

I guess the point to that verse is that it would be really insanely crazy to keep track of how many hairs are on everyone's head. So, God must be crazy in love with us, huh?

Now, look at verse 8 and circle the thing that Jesus does for us because of His crazy love for us! **Fill in the blank below:**

"If anyone . . . . . . . . . . . . . . . . . . . . . . . . . . . . . . . . . . . . . . . . . . . me publicly here

on earth, I, the Son of Man, will openly. . . . . . . . . . . . . . . . . . . . . . . . . . . . . . . . . . . .

that person in the presence of God's angels."

Jesus said that He "acknowledges us" in the presence of God's angels. When Jesus' words were actually recorded, they were written in Greek. What He really said was "I will openly homologeo [you] in the presence of God's angels." That Greek word means "to speak out freely!"

He talks about you! He wants to. It freely flows out of His mouth. (Kind of like when you find a new friend and can't wait to tell her about Him.) He is totally telling all the angels and God the Father about you.

Wait. Jesus is talking about you? Really?

Yes, really! Even when Jesus was on this earth praying for His twelve closest friends, He was also praying for Y-O-U! He said so Himself. Check it out. **Circle the word that represents both you and me if you have asked Jesus to live in your heart.**

### JOHN 17:20

"I am praying not only for these disciples but also for all

who will ever believe in me because of their testimony."

Did His prayers end when He ascended into heaven? No way! **Circle the word on page 65 that tells you how long He'll be praying for you.**

## HEBREWS 7:25

"Therefore he is able, once and forever, to save

everyone who comes to God through him. He lives forever to

plead with God on their behalf."

He will be praying for you forever! That's a long, long time. And make no mistake who He's talking to. **Circle who *all* this "free speaking" about you is directed to.**

## ROMANS 8:34

" . . . he is the one who died for us and was

raised to life for us and is sitting at the place of highest

honor next to God, pleading for us."

It feels wonderful to know that Jesus is talkin' about you and me to God the Father! Guess what? Jesus likes it when we approach our friendship with Him the same way. Go back to our main passage from Luke and find the word that is highlighted. **Write it in *big letters* below.**

. . . . . . . . . . . . . . . . . . . . . . . . . . . . . . . . . . . . . . . . . . . . . . . . .

*If* we speak out freely for Him, then He will speak out freely for us! The gift of God's love and salvation is free. To live in His constant protection and provision depends at least in part on how much we live for Him. Are you talking *about* Him? Are you freely speaking about Him in front of friends, family, and classmates?

# SKG Puzzle Craze
## Our A-MAZE-ing Jesus!

Here are some fun and easy ways to "speak out freely" for Jesus!
**Help Secret Keeper Girl Toni find her way to God's throne by choosing to do simple things that speak out for Jesus.**

start

Invite Toni to church.

Carry your Bible to school.

Take Toni to an SKG Tour stop.

Wear a T-shirt that says "I love Jesus!"

Pray quietly beside her at lunchtime.

Send her a note with a Bible verse.

finish

Answer on page 77

**1** **At the top of each of these columns, write the name of at least one friend who you know has never really met Jesus.** This person isn't "friends" with Him. (If you think all of your friends know Jesus, go ahead and write the names of some of them. We should be helping them grow closer to our Best Friend, Jesus!)

1. . . . . . . . . . . . . . . . . . 2. . . . . . . . . . . . . . . . . . 3. . . . . . . . . . . . . . . . . . . .

**②** What have you done to tell them about Jesus?

.............................................................

.............................................................

.............................................................

.............................................................

**③** What do you think God wants you to do to tell them about Jesus?
**Using the box with your friends' names, go ahead and write in some ideas.**

### Reach up To Talk to God

OK. Are you ready for this? I'm going to let you write your whole letter to God today. No help at all. Just look in your heart and ask Him how you can pray the Scripture verses you just studied into your life. Ready? Go!

Dear. ...............................................

.............................................................

.............................................................

.............................................................

.............................................................

.............................................................

.............................................................

..........................................................................

..........................................................................

..........................................................................

..........................................................................

..........................................................................

..........................................................................

..........................................................................

..........................................................................

..........................................................................

..........................................................................

..........................................................................

..........................................................................

..........................................................................

..........................................................................

In Jesus' Name,

..........................................................................

(SIGN HERE)

## SKG Puzzle Craze

*Crazy-for-Jesus coupons*

It's actually easy to share your love for Jesus. You just show kindness and do it in His name. Here's an easy way to do it. **Pick four people to bless with these cool coupons.** Just ask God to help you decide who you can give them to, and present them as soon as possible.

# Get Well Soon!

MISSED YOU at school today, and here are some **highs** and *lows* that you missed. *I'm praying for you.*

**Assignments:** . . . . . . . . . . . . . . . . . . . . . . . . . . . . . . . . . . . . . . . . . . . . . . . . . . . . . . . . . . . . . . . . . . . . . . . . . . . . . . . . . . . . . . . . . . . . . . . . . . . . . . . . . . . . . . . . . . . . . . . . . . . . . . . . . . . . . . . . . . . . . . . . . . . . . . . . . . . . . . . . . . . . . . . . . . . . . . . . . . . . . . . . . . . . . . . . . . . . . . . . . . . . . . . . . . . . . . . . . . . . . . . . . . . . . . . . . . . . . . . . . . . . . . . . . .

**News (Highs & Lows):** . . . . . . . . . . . . . . . . . . . . . . . . . . . . . . . . . . . . . . . . . . . . . . . . . . . . . . . . . . . . . . . . . . . . . . . . . . . . . . . . . . . . . . . . . . . . . . . . . . . . . . . . . . . . . . . . . . . . . . . . . . . . . . . . . . . . . . . . . . . . . . . . . . . . . . . . . . . . . . . . . . . . . . . . . . . . . . . . . . . . . . . . . . . . . . . . . .

*"And [Jesus] healed people who had every kind of sickness and disease." (Matthew 4:23)*

To: . . . . . . . . . . . . . . . . . . . . . . . . . . . . . .

From: . . . . . . . . . . . . . . . . . . . . . . . . . . .

Secret Keeper GIRL

**friends!**

To: .....................

From: ...................

*Get Well S...*

# Look, It's a Book!

**Hey,** just wanted to loan you my fav *Secret Keeper Girl* fiction book! It's **funny** and easy to read, but it has some great advice about friendship in it. *Meet:*

...... **Toni**

..... **Kate**

..... **Yuzi**

..... **Danika**

*"Whoever walks with the wise will become wise; whoever walks with fools will suffer harm."*
(Proverbs 13:20)

# To the Rescue!

**Having a hard day?** Hand this coupon in anytime for help. Just check one and hand this in and I will:

...... clean your desk out for you.

...... help you study.

...... pick up your room.

...... pray with you.

*"A friend is always loyal, and a brother is born to help in time of need." (Proverbs 17:17)*

Secret Keeper GiRL

To: ..............................

From: ..........................

*sweet!*

**Secret Keeper GIRL**

To: ....................

From: ....................

*Born to Help!*

# Sweet Surprise!

**Here's a candy bar that's as sweet as you are.**

Have a great day, friend!

*"The heartfelt counsel of a friend is as sweet as perfume and incense." (Proverbs 27:9)*

# Do You Know Jesus?

I remember the day that I began my friendship with Jesus. I was four and a half years old. I was at a neighborhood Bible club where I had just heard that Jesus loved me and had died for me on the cross.

### JOHN 3:16 SAYS:

"For God so loved the world that he gave his only Son, so that everyone

who believes in him will not perish but have eternal life."

The teacher told me that the reason Jesus had to die is because God is pure and holy and perfect and can't be near anything that is not. So, He can't be near sin. (Sinning is doing something bad or against God's plan.)

### ROMANS 3:23

"For all have sinned and fall short of God's glorious standard."

Any sin—even just one little one—separates us from God's perfection. I didn't want that. But I knew I had sinned. I wanted to live forever in heaven with Jesus, so I prayed a prayer that sounded a little like this:

"Dear Jesus:

I know I have sinned. I know that this means I cannot live with You in heaven forever. I also know that You died to take the punishment for my sins. Will You forgive me? Come into my heart and be the God of my life. From this day forward, I want to be Your friend.

In Jesus' Name,
Amen!"

I still remember what things were like that day. I remember the crack in the sidewalk that I saw as I prayed with my eyes open. I remember the smell of the evergreen trees nearby. I treasure that memory and I know it was the beginning of my friendship with Jesus.

If you have never prayed a prayer like that, you can do it right now. Go get your mom or a teacher if you want someone to pray with you. But don't delay. Jesus wants to be your Best Friend!

appendix B

# How To Use "My Best Friend, Jesus" Bible Study

You can do this Secret Keeper Girl Bible study all alone if you want to. But we have some other ideas for you in case you'd like to be creative:

**Mother/Daughter Bible Study**

Your mom will learn as much as you will.
You see, it's not me teaching, it's God. His Spirit is fully capable of helping your mom to meditate in a way that teaches her as she leads you. To do this with your mom, just get two copies and dig in. You can do it once a week or you can do it every day for a week.

**Small Group or Sunday School**

How fun would it be to discuss all the great things you learn each week? You can do that by grabbing a group of friends to do this with. Do it after school once a week or in Sunday school every Sunday. We like to keep things simple with Secret Keeper Girl Bible studies, so you really don't need any extra books. If you are the leader, just select one appropriate question from each of the three sections:

- Dig in to Study
- Look Inside Yourself
- Reach up to Pray

*Be sure to enjoy some fun snacks at the beginning and to end in prayer!*

# ♥ ♥ Puzzle Answers

**Page 13:** ACROSS: 2 Confident, 3 Obedient, 5 Understanding. DOWN: 1 Successful, 2 Comforted, 4 Strong

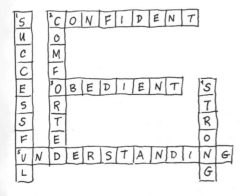

**Page 21:** Prison, Left Jobs, Beatings, Death, Left Families

```
A B     N B R I N O T I G T I
P E E E E I E O S B G N P I N
R E L A R   S I L M I S T A F
I E E P T I (L E F T   J O B S)
S O F O R I F   A L G   L I E
O N T P E I N E I I A F E R I
O E   L O P B G S I S A N H E
N S J F   E I D A E T H T H S
T J O A S J D E A T L A F B S
  S M E O   N T I S E M I T F
L (B E A T I N G S) D L N A M N
A I L E F T   F E M I L I E S
E (L E F T   F A M I L I E S) G
L F R F L E F T   J O B J L D
S J S O O F M O E A E A F E
```

**Page 31:** Jesus loved Martha, Mary, and Lazarus!

**Page 37:** Insulted, Mad, Infuriated, Resentful, Jealous, Offended

**Page 47:**

| 1 | 2 | 3 | 4 | 5 |
|---|---|---|---|---|
| Peter Denies Jesus | Jesus Dies on the Cross | Jesus Is Buried in a Tomb | Jesus Rises from the Dead | Jesus Meets Peter |

**Page 55:** ACROSS: 3 Joy, 4 Kindness, 5 Peace, 6 Self-Control. DOWN: 1 Goodness, 2 Gentleness, 7 Love

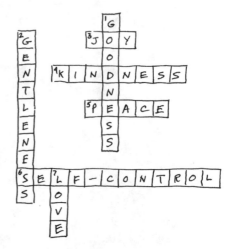

**Page 66:** Maze

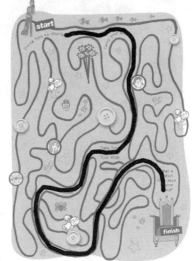

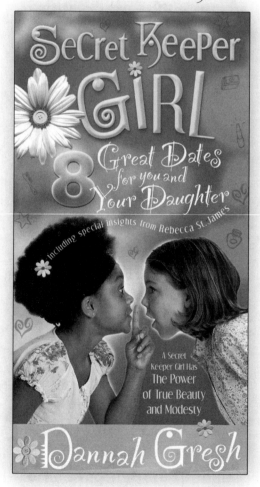

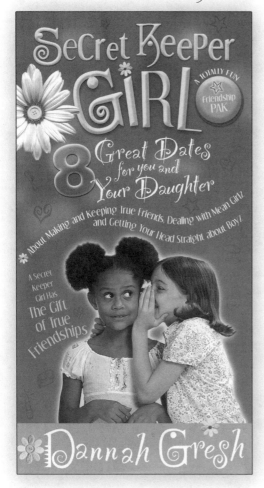

# MORE

## SeCret Keeper GIRL

find out more at...

## SecretKeeperGirl.com

1-800-678-6928 • MOODYPUBLISHERS.COM